IF YO

PLAY, PLAY.

DON'T PLAY!

And Other Words of Wisdom to
Amuse, Bemuse, Confuse, and Defuse

from the Astonishing Mind of

STEPHEN F. KAUFMAN

HWP

Hanshi Warrior Press
"...words that matter"

If You're Gonna Play, Play. Don't Play! –
And Other Words of Wisdom to Amuse, Bemuse,
Confuse, and Defuse

Kaufman, Stephen F, 1939 –
apothegms, quotations, sayings, homilies, wisdom,
philosophy, adages

ISBN-13: 978-1530511037
ISBN-10: 1530511038

Hanshi Warrior Press
PO Box 135, Lenox Hill
New York, NY 10021
hanshibooks@gmail.com
www.hanshi.com

First Edition and First Printing March, 2016
1 3 5 7 9 10 8 6 4 2

Dedication

To everyone with a sense of humor,
a sense of ponder, a sense of huh,
a sense of duh, a sense of calm,
and a good sense of self.

Preface

This book comprises the sayings heard by Hanshi's students on a daily basis. That the master comes up with them, seemingly out of nowhere, is indicative of his amazing presence of mind. He is never at a loss for words, and he himself doesn't give much thought to them except once in a while when he is surprised at what he has just said.

There are more than 500 apothegms in this edition. Hanshi thinks there will probably be around ten thousand before he is finished. He also knows that some are to be laughed at, some looked askance at, some sneered at, or whatever else your reaction to them could be. He isn't really concerned about that, considering that he has to walk around with his own head all day, every day. Aren't you lucky that you don't have to? Enjoy them for what they are.

Beware the consequences of choice—you always get what you pay for.

An anonymous student

...and, from the master's own voice:

"I could not stand being me
if I wasn't who I am."
SFK

1. Make sure you know what you want even when you think you do.

2. All things come to those who wait, especially those in a hurry.

3. Everything is a complete and total success, including failure.

4. You don't have to ask for what is already yours. But don't steal that which isn't.

5. Stress and strain come to those who don't know they don't need it.

6. Burn your bridges behind you and let those left behind come forth if they want to.

7. You have never been wrong in your life even when you think you were.

8. All is one if you accept your Self.

9. Clever technique should be avoided. The resultant arrogance will betray you.

10. Hoping is based on non-acceptance. Wishful thinking is willful denial.

11. Write your own bible. You already know the truth.

12. Practice what you don't know. If you're sincere, you'll find you already do.

13. Familiarity should breed intent more than contempt.

14. Stupid people work at it. So do geniuses.

15. A good idea isn't yours alone; it must be given away ... for the right price.

16. If you constantly sharpen your knife, you'll eventually cut yourself.

17. Think something up by yourself, for yourself, and as yourself.

18. Say 'thank you' even when you mean it.

19. Sincere imitation is the greatest form of flattery, but flattery without sincerity is the worst kind of insult.

20. Demand from life that which you know you deserve.

21. Politically correct people ain't. They hide their true feelings.

22. Be the personification of the ideal. Do not become the personification of the ideal.

23. Move in harmony with your enemy and he will become your ally.

24. Never be right for the wrong reasons.

25. The intelligent direction of will delivers all things, not will power which debilitates reason.

26. Constantly practice your art and be its master; otherwise, you will be its slave and give it up.

27. When you don't make up your mind, you already have.

28. Mind your own business, and if you don't have any, get some.

29. You will now or you won't later.

30. Be conscious of your bad habits. They're the same as everyone else's.

31. Worrying about the end of the world will be the end of 'your' world.

32. Business is **not** war. There is a significant difference in not getting a deal compared to having your head cut off.

33. Freedom is its own trap, and traps induce creativity—if you let it happen.

34. When you recognize yourself in your enemies, forgive them, but not what they did and learn from it.

35. The oneness of all is everything, including your ego.

36. If you raise your prices, raise your quality. Actually, if you raise your quality, the prices will raise themselves.

37. Raise your consciousness by accepting yourself as already perfect.

38. Bad habits are good to break, even if you enjoy them.

39. You are the sum total of all the thoughts you have ever had—even some you haven't had.

40. If you're gonna play, play. Don't play!

41. Regardless of good intentions, most people only mean well for themselves.

42. Humiliation may be necessary, especially when you're outnumbered.

43. If you don't do it right, you can't do it wrong.

44. If your work is that secret, then you probably aren't doing anything.

45. Don't tell others where to go if you don't know where it's at.

46. Those who can benefit from a good arrangement are usually the first to complain.

47. If you want a free ride, buy a ticket!

48. Feeling bad for hurting someone is easier than apologizing, but not as good.

49. Just because you look good going in doesn't mean you'll look good coming out.

50. Be good to as many people as you can rather than being nice; you'll never know when you'll need them.

51. If you don't share your luck, no one will share your misfortune.

52. There is no honor among thieves unless you find one you can trust.

53. Never base your happiness on the opinions of others, or both will control you.

54. If you ain't happy here, you ain't gonna be happy there.

55. Watch where you're going and not where you've been or, for that matter, where you're at.

56. No matter how exalted you think your throne is, you always end up sitting on your ass.

57. If you talk shit, be sure to bring lots of toilet paper.

58. When you fuss with a snake, you get the fangs.

59. Never confuse an act of compassion as a demonstration of weakness.

60. Very few people can overcome the tragedy of their own inconsequence.

61. Intelligence is no excuse for intelligence.

62. Use force when it is necessary to ensure that no force is necessary.

63. Make your own decisions and you won't make as many mistakes.

64. Madness among great ones is to be expected, but make sure you're mad and not nuts.

65. Flattery will get you something you will eventually deserve—a swift kick in your ass.

66. Better to never hear about something than never to hear the end of it.

67. What you see is what you hear, especially when you're reading.

68. If anything is anything, then everything is everything.

69. Constantly re-evaluate your net worth, but don't include money.

70. Cutting through is better than slashing at.

71. Being intelligent and being smart is not the same thing regardless of how brilliant you are.

72. Watch out for people who operate with their feet firmly planted in the air.

73. Heed your own counsel, or you might need another's counsel.

74. There is no such thing as 110%. As well, there is never anything less than 100%.

75. Freebies are never appreciated and they cost you too much.

76. People who attain to greatness appear insincere. Ask the insincere.

77. Don't worry about making enemies. Everyone does it with ease.

78. Don't work hard. Work smart and let the other guy grunt.

79. If information doesn't come from actual fact, consider the appropriateness of the rumor.

80. Be lenient towards the mistakes of others, maybe, but do not be indulgent.

81. Do what you tell yourself to do and don't take no for an answer.

82. Make sure your victories don't cost too much.

83. Make your associates think they're important even if they are.

84. You do not enhance your understanding of anything by gloating over another' s failure.

85. Most people can't stand being who they are because they can't stand being what they are.

86. Many are controlled by the one through the few, with the rare exception of you.

87. Reality is neither subjective nor objective. It simply is.

88. Just because you play notes on the piano doesn't mean you can play music.

89. Idiocy to you may be intelligence to someone else.
Try it the other way around.

90.Give your kids everything they want, and they'll never give you anything you need.

91. When someone tells you half a truth, it's a complete lie.

92. Squeaky wheels don't always get the grease—sometimes they get replaced.

93. Information is not knowledge, but you can make it that if you're smart.

94. What you really don't know is what you don't believe, but what you really know is real.

95. Do what you deem necessary for the propagation of your own mythology.

96. Annihilate the authority of good and evil and do what is correct for circumstance.

97. Suffer the eradication of guilt and self-imposed nihilism.

98. The abolition of desire is based on acceptance: acknowledgement of having and not wanting, thereby making pursuance a needless exertion.

99. Sense your own joy of being lest you become a walking irrelevancy.

100. It is better to use your head before you use your hands or your heart.

101. Don't be proud of what you've learned, or you will soon forget what you know.

102. The bigger the words, the smaller the idea.

103. Clever people have little self-esteem; they're always looking to jive someone.

104. When you keep it only to yourself, you may not really have it to give to others.

105. See if you can think no evil for five minutes. Don't feel guilty if you can't.

106. The more suspicious you are, you're right!

107. Don't let your ego be fed with egotism unless you're an egotist. Or is it egoist?

108. Concentrate on your work, and your work won't constipate on you.

109. The fewer the words, the more intense the meaning.

110. Demand clarity of thought for clarity of purpose; then you'll know what you want.

111. Ask with authority and conviction, but first demand the answer from your Self.

112. Look at the books on your shelf and they'll tell you who you think you are.

113. To understand your art more fully, consider how silly it is to pursue it.

114. Practice your art with conviction; you'll be more convincing and won't get convicted.

115. To properly work it out, first work it in.

116. If you keep resting, you will never be arresting.

117. Thank your self for a job well done, but don't cop an attitude.

118. Pay attention to the truth and you won't have to think about the consequences.

119. There is no such thing as the fastest gun in the West. Ask Wild Bill.

120. Center yourself around everything and control it all from within.

121. People will believe in anything that works even when it doesn't.

122. If you think first, you won't have to think later.

123. Nothing is total without complement, including you. No-thing is!

124. The two most powerful words in the universe are "I AM." They are also the weakest.

125. The pictures on a man's wall may be nothing more than colors to him.

126. Do not look for meaning in meaningless things, such as words of wisdom.

127. Sweet music to you may be noise to someone else.

128. Don't be afraid of change; it's the only thing you can depend on.

129. There is no end to wisdom until you say there is.

130. Many fools speak the truth even if they don't know they do.

131. Hostile people do not like themselves; however, they are in love with themselves.

132. Don't rely on what **they** say. **They** are generally jive and sometimes you are **they** too.

133. Conquering your fears is the only victory worth having—so is conquering your joys.

134. If you only think of beating others, you will eventually beat yourself.

135. If you think about the question, you can generally figure the answer out for yourself.

136. People with too much pride are usually hiding something.

137. The true way in life is unknown; so is the untrue.

138. Don't worry that beauty is only skin deep. Be your own proctologist.

139. Listen to the words people use to limit themselves, but don't laugh—wise guy!

140. Never boast of your luck in front of losers—or behind them.

141. It doesn't matter what you think or do. You're right or wrong, anyway.

142. No problems exist; therefore, nothing must be resolved–unless you're a troublemaker.

143. Just because you seek justice doesn't mean you'll get it; you may get busted instead.

144. Don't consider the rewards of your work, and the results will be better.

145. Insist that Heaven unfold for you, and it will—or it won't.

146. Circumstance does not withhold anything truly desired except what you think you want, but not what you know you want.

147. If you can only give and not take, you don't appreciate giving.

148. Be the woman and the man, and then you can love and govern without consideration.

149. To be in favor or in disgrace is the same thing, based on your perception.

150. The only man qualified to rule is the one who sees all people as the same except himself.

151. Understand unity and you will understand separateness.

152. Attention should never create a tension.

153. Do not expect the Universe to show special favor. It already has. It created **you.**

154. If it's heavy and slows you down, you've become a target. Dump it!

155. Good teachers reveal only that which is already known; bad teachers force opinion.

156. Enjoy the food and friendship, but don't use your sleeve as a napkin.

157. By thinking someone is a fool, you will think you are more learned than they. Wrong!

158. Don't compete; create! It makes your brain work better.

159. Wind doesn't blow forever and rains eventually cease, even if it's your house that's getting flooded.

160. It is wise to honor others to others, not to themselves.

161. When you pat yourself on the back, you can't work with both hands.

162. The balance of things depends upon lightness and 'wait.'

163. Don't permit your view to block your vision.

164. Don't display your skills to impress the crowd, or you'll start thinking you're important.

165. Do not think that virtue is the only good. So-called bad is also perfection.

166. A wise man will somehow know a foolish man can be beneficial to him.

167. To be one thing, also be the opposite, and that way you will understand completeness.

168. When you see a man in his glory, know that he has known or will know shame.

169. The earth will always survive to serve its own nature, but don't litter anyway.

170. Heaven does not know good or evil. It only knows perfection; therefore, neither exists.

171. A wise man knows when to proceed and when not to, forcing nothing according to whim.

172. Men cost more than weapons and that's why kings don't last.

174. When you attain success, you also attain grief.

173. The accomplishment of a goal is the accomplishment of the goal—not the paycheck.

175. If men knew the name of God, God would have no need to exist.

176. Conquer yourself and you will be powerful. Conquer others and you're only a fool.

177. Life lasts forever if you decide it does, but don't question the form.

178. To perish quickly, think only of yourself.

179. Greatness spreads its wealth without restriction—except to you. Right?

180. There is never a need to want, only a need to accept.

181. **Not concerned with profit, your work will flow with ease. That's profit.**

182. **Morality is real when it is expressed as virtue and not previously thought about.**

183. **In power and quickness is strength and speed.**

184. **Time stands still if you stop stopping.**

185. Sunshine follows the warrior even when it is raining.

186. Water penetrates the hardest stone even when it's diverted, as all gives way to persistence.

187. Which costs more? Gain or loss?

188. Beware the paradox of sages looking like idiots and idiots appearing wise. Or, is it the other way?

189. The Way of the Universe is celeritous. Look it up. What do you think? Do you?

190. When you know where you want to go, you're there.

191. You only know love if you know hate. It is best to know neither but simply to be.

192. Death is a meaningless event that takes you to your next self-defined place, which is an incorrect assumption in the best of cases.

193. God is obedient to all things. If that isn't true, then you aren't here.

194. Give life to things, but don't seek to own them. Give death to things, but don't seek to own them either.

195. Do not seek to command; seek to teach. Do not seek to obey; seek to understand. When you do, you will.

196. To be in your right mind, go out of it, but don't lose your house keys.

197. People with attitudes are usually the ones that shouldn't have them.

198. Royalty suggests arrogance until it is overthrown by humility, then again becoming arrogance.

199. Think deeply and you won't be shallow.

200. The more you govern, the cleverer your people become— including how they cheat on their taxes.

201. Do not be deceived by the appearances of the enemy's armor— or his attaché case.

202. Good fortune can be quelled by bad behavior, even though bad behavior is sometimes virtuous.

203. Don't build statues to yourself with your own dung; but, if you do, make sure not to step in it.

204. When governing, look down from above by being level headed.

205. Things flow from top to bottom. That is the nature of things. Sometimes they flow from bottom to top.

206. Good men have wealth to share; evil men only have riches to hoard.

207. Give people the presence you would like to get from them.

208. Permit nothing to enter your thoughts except the illusion of your desire.

209. Never make promises that are too easy to keep. It's too hard to do.

210. Act without action and the future can be foreseen, but it is better to keep busy.

211. Never want things of no value— they are too costly.

212. Consider the care given to the project and the value of your output—then, raise your prices.

213. It is better to take the easy way in rather than the easy way out. Consider taking neither and just go through.

214. It is much easier to rule by simply suggesting what is desired—and not getting it, anyway.

215. There are no secrets to reveal except your own.

216. Reality and appearance are both the same: illusion based on delusion, which is really allusion.

217. Don't talk down. Talk up–and don't blame the fates!

218. Draw your sword without taking it out of the scabbard–but make sure it's sharp.

219. Think well of yourself and let that be your answer.

220. The executioner is a master at chopping off heads. Imitators chop off their own hands.

221. The walls of the house contain the useful space—if you don't put up too many shelves.

222. The strong and mighty may topple, which is no better or worse than "flakes" floating to heaven.

223. Enlightened men always have enough; their abundance increases, as does their desire.

224. Make sure the fire of your passion doesn't burn your heart out.

225. Paradox is its own virtue. Isn't that not the truth?

226. Cleverness is based on not knowing. You follow my drift?

227. Wise men do not hoard their possessions. They rid themselves of the weight and then get more.

228. Knowers are not the learned, just as the learned are not necessarily the knowers.

229. There is no need for profit and gain, since it is all lost in the end regardless of your will and testament.

230. Too many books cause confusion—except the ones you write.

231. Use minimum effort for maximum effect—or work hard and get nowhere.

232. You are the sum total of all of the thoughts that have ever been, whether you like it or not.

233. No one is responsible for your fallacies, probably not even yourself.

234. If you really want it, you have to really want it and not feel guilty about getting it.

235. If something bothers you, deny it authority in your life; that way you can make room for something else to bother you.

236. Ease and grace ... do it all with ease and grace even doing that with ease and grace.

237. Will power doesn't last, but will will.

238. Accept the fact that you are perfect, just the way you are. Now, change for the better!

239. Spirit will do if the mind insists that the body conform—unless you're neurotic.

240. Nothing exists in a vacuum except other people's ideas, especially when they don't conform to yours.

241. If you want to know something, learn it and then teach it. You may end up knowing it.

242. With teamwork you always have people on your side even when you're wrong.

243. Money is not the root of all evil, but the junk it buys usually is.

244. Never beg anyone's pardon. They may have caused the problem.

245. If advice cannot be changed, it isn't based in reality except for what you tell others.

246. Lovers shouldn't go to bed angry, but rather mad for each other.

247. The less men think, the more they think they do.

248. If you can't get mad at friends, they aren't friends.

249. Read with understanding and retention and then forget it; it will be there when you need it.

250. Real heroes get up and go to work every day, but their kids don't necessarily know that.

251. Don't find fault until you find a reason for it.

252. The secret of success is conviction and devotion to purpose—your own!

253. If you think too much, you won't get anything done.

254. If your conscience is clear, so is the traffic jam in front of you.

255. Dragons don't go after butterflies unless there's nothing else to eat.

256. Brag about your friend's accomplishments, and he'll share his joy if he likes himself.

257. If the door is locked, use your *ki.*

258. Everything has its value, even if it's useless.

259. People make assumptions so they can have a reference point for their own consciousness.

260. Rumors are based on others wanting your space for themselves because they don't handle their own.

261. Be sure you're right, and then proceed—even if you're wrong.

262. Turn your enemies into suckers by letting them think they've won.

263. When you need help you will generally get it, but not necessarily when you want it.

264. When you cease to be, your works will still be evident—for the time being.

265. Absence makes the hear go ponder.

266. Cure your dis-ease and you will cure your disease.

267. Make sure the rules you change don't create other rules you will have to follow.

268. Your imagination is God talking to you. How lucky can you get?

269. Visualization is the art of seeing that which should be, but ain't. Redefine your mistakes.

270. Listen to the affectations in a man's speech rather than his words.

271. Put passion into everything you do, or you'll burn yourself out.

272. Everything yields to persistence, including you.

273. To really get up, really get down.

274. Have abundance in all things, including moderation.

275. The only competitor you should have is you. You can always beat him.

276. Study one thing thoroughly and you'll get insight into everything, including yourself.

277. Don't be afraid to be perfect. You never will be, anyway.

278. Words of wisdom are ever for sale. Buy this book now!

279. Don't seek involvement if you only want participation.

280. True friends are hard to come by; so are untrue friends: both are subject to change.

281. Focus on principles, not politics.

282. Competition will always interfere with the pure creative expression of your idea.

283. A man who truly sees sameness in things sees difference in all.

284. A wise king takes from his people what he needs to rule and gives back the rest so that he can get more later.

285. If you retire from the world and hide in a cave, you still have to deal with the park rangers.

286. If you're so damned smart, how come you only have money?

287. Once you start looking cool, that's what you're doing.

288. Dispel your own mythology and you'll find out how important you really are.

289. Beware the hideous weight of responsibility. Relish it; you'll get more done.

290. When you know where you want to be, you are.

291. Make believe you really exist.

292. If you haven't got time for someone with something important for both of you, then you haven't got time to waste time, either.

293. Don't be humble ... you're not that great.

294. Many people can't read because most people can't write. Do you understand this prioritized and preevaluated parameter?

295. Understand your life strategy, but be aware of the similarities between your desires and your actuality.

296. Never confuse profit with profitability.

297. If you see nothing wrong with anything you have ever done, you obviously have nothing to learn. Lie down—you're dead.

298. The lack of understanding one's own true worth is the cause of all dissension.

299. Dig yourself, or you won't be dug!

300. Never choose cheap goods. They're too costly.

301. Exercise is the physical diversion we use to interfere with our ignorance interfering with our non-acceptance of perfection.

302. Reward is a virtue of accomplishment and not a causation of it.

303. False fears create weaknesses, as imaginary situations create difficulties.

304. Life is a game and, therefore, it must not be taken seriously.

305. The heart is essential if the intellect is to understand what the spirit is.

306. Difficulties in life lie in being unable to accept yourself as complete and perfect without having to practice.

307. Every man's work is the same. Doing it or not takes the same amount of energy.

308. It is easier to understand the difficult than the simple.

309. Familiarity breeds intent more than it breeds contempt.

310. If you're critical of things, try seeing the overall picture; if you don't, you'll miss it all.

311. If you're polite, some people become arrogant; if you're nasty, they become self-righteous.

312. If you know what you want but can't put it into words, then you don't know what you want.

313. If you see it, you're not doing it; if you're doing it, you don't see it: this has nothing to do with observation, but awareness.

314. People with nothing to say always have something to say.

315. Purely selfish people have no time for attitudes. They're too busy working to enhance their own lives.

316. People who stand on ceremony usually miss the parade.

317. Humble opinions are based on the idea that you don't know what you're talking about.

318. Think about what you are saying. Read the dictionary!

319. You always get what you want, but only when you want it.

320. Coincidence is a result of planned obsolescence. Think about it.

321. It isn't what you want for yourself as much as it is what you ask yourself for.

322. When you wish upon a star, it is usually the star that gets what you want.

323. It's only important if it matters.

324. Exceptions to the rule ain't. They are the rule.

325. Expect the unexpected by expecting the expected.

326. Instead of to be or not to be, try to neither be nor not to be.

327. Accept all the good you get even if you can recognize it as such.

328. Focus and concentration are only words. Pay attention to what I just said!

329. If change does not occur, nothing will remain the same anyway.

330. Most people thrive on ennui.

331. The line between yin and yang is not a combination of both: it is neither of each.

332. Walking on fire is a parlor trick, but not walking on fire is the real thing!

333. Do not permit arrogance to confuse you or permit conceit to deceit you. Now—proceit!

334. If your goose is cooked, you can't honk.

335. Never be afraid of making mistakes—that's all you'll probably ever do anyway.

336. It is not the technique; it is the intention.

337. If you have it, you probably don't want it.

338. Do the best you can. You might find out you're something else!

339. Knowing about something is not the same thing as knowing it.

340. It is easy to praise, difficult to admonish, but necessary to admonish to be able to praise.

341. Don't get mad—get paid.

342. The power of a prophecy has nothing to do with it being true or false.

343. Jealous people have no idea of their own worth.

344. Understanding does not imply agreement, as disagreement does not imply understanding.

345. There is a distinct difference between genuine knowledge and personal opinion.

346. Judge the work and not the man, especially if he's making you think.

347. If you disagree with something, have a reason—even more so if you agree.

348. Are you well read, or quantity read?

349. Anytime you use a word to describe an action, you are using a word to describe an action.

350. Do not permit your ego to interfere with your ascensions.

351. Risks are based on errors in judgment due to non-committal acceptance.

352. The challenge is to be able to let the question answer itself.

353. Some of whatever you do must be fiction because your life is based on the fantasy you create.

354. Cowards will always accuse you of non-benevolence.

355. If perfection was simple to attain, it would have no value.

356. Clever technique should be avoided because it gives you a false sense of security, and the arrogance will betray you.

357. A laugh a day is not enough; however, don't get carried away!

358. You must make a friend of death, because if you don't, it will laugh at you.

359. Hope is the anesthesia of the people.

360. Wisdom is cheap. Ask anyone who knows everything.

361. A soul is require3d for dealing with and allaying the fears of the unknown.

362. When you know you know, you know.

363. Leniency leads to indulgence, which is the first step towards weakness.

364. If you go for distance, you miss the scenery.

365. Do you make the choices, or do the choices make you?

366. It is best to know things before you think you do; therefore, you won't have to think you do at all.

367. If you don't consider the needs of those you vanquish, you will have to consider the needs of those you vanquish.

368. Don't degrade yourself by putting on an act for fools.

369. You shouldn't think about new ways of thinking about old ideas with old ideas about thinking about new ways.

370. Be inevitable!

371. Most people have no time to learn something new because they're too busy being confused with what they do know.

372. Take it ... easy.

373. When you take the magic carpet ride, remember to bring a vacuum cleaner.

374. Don't put on an act. Put on a show!

375. Difficulties exist because you don't think things should occur with ease.

376. If you aren't part of the decision, you're part of the derision.

377. Never confuse meaning with definition.

378. Focus on substance, not meaningless rhetoric and distracting metaphor.

379. It doesn't matter how tight you think your shit is. Everybody gets diarrhea.

380. People will do whatever they have to do in order not to do what they have to do.

381. How you derive yourself is how you arrive yourself.

382. If you surround yourself with stuff that's hip, you ain't.

383. Stop thinking in terms of being less important than you really are.

384. Patience is not a virtue; it is a tool you need when dealing with non-decisive procrastination.

385. It is necessary to understand the requirements of a goal only when you determine its importance.

386. Weak-minded people will always seek to destroy that which they cannot attain to.

387. Be aware the *karmady* of errors.

388. Light drawn back into the eyes dims the illumination of the vision.

389. The slower you go, the faster you are. Be quick about it!

390. If you don't go through, you are!

391. Make no distinction between heart and mind. Without one, neither exists.

392. Just because you think you're right doesn't mean you aren't.

393. Be in the primal state on a sophisticated level.

394. When the good go bad, even the devil runs for cover.

395. If you.re not in control, you can't be in charge. If you're in charge, it doesn't mean you're in control.

396. Don't make excuses for weakness by being arrogant.

397. You can't ride two horses with one ass.

398. Be smart enough to be smart enough to know that others may be smarter than you.

399. Dream your dreams and live them. They're not yours anyway; so, you have nothing to lose.

400. Let your enlightenment be fueled by the ignorance of the masses.

401. Dig your self doing it.
Don't do it to dig yourself.

402. Don't let 'em know you're
coming. Let 'em know you've been
there.

403. Don't dance unless there's
music. You'll look like a fool.

404. Liberality breeds intemperance,
as indulgence breeds greed.

405. It is not your educational degree; it is your degree of education.

406. Be audacious, but not presumptuous; bold, but not impertinent.

407. Every orthodoxy is its own heresy.

408. If it is not enhancing your life, it is limiting your life.

409. If you are not swift in your decisions, it will become necessary to maintain a defensive position at all times.

410. No matter what choice you make, you're either right or wrong.

411. There is no such thing as yin and yang, which is not to suggest that yin and yang do not exist.

412. It is advantageous to be enlightened, as long as you aren't incandescent.

413. It is better to be mysterious rather than enigmatic.

414. Hope is based on wishful thinking and is a limitation of acceptance.

415. Don't define anything, especially those things you use to define your definitions.

416. You can't be here if you want to be out there; you can't be out there if you stay stuck in here.

417. The more you accept from life, the more you have to give to have to give.

418. A man moves forward in any direction, including backwards.

419. The funniest thing you will ever see is yourself–naked–in the mirror–with or without your clothes on.

420. Do not become litherous–regardless of your good motives.

421. Survival is simply a matter of being able to change bad habits at the right time.

422. Do not become enamored of your delusion; you will become impoverished by it, and that will be your legacy.

423. If you're doing something and you're not on fire, then you're just blowing smoke.

424. It's not how much things cost to acquire them, but rather how much it costs not to.

425. Let go of the self, the most difficult of easy things to do.

426. Knowing little, you control much information; having much information, you have little knowledge.

427. Do not seek to control others or seek to let others control you.

428. When you manipulate power, you bring about destruction. When you illuminate power, you bring about profound blessings.

429. When you know what you are doing, people will always find fault. When you act like you know what you're doing, people will acknowledge you as a master.

430. . Heavies keep their heavy by being light about it.

431. The way of a warrior is fraught with terror that can only be overcome with love of the self.

432. Beware the indefinable stupidity of common sense.

433. Develop a mentality of non-invasiveness and accept it into your mind with ease: protect yourself from all things at all times—good, bad, or indifferent.

434. Few people know what people are saying because they don't know what they themselves mean.

435. If you're gonna carry on, make sure you can carry it off.

436. Enlightenment sucks ... the life right out of you!

437. If you don't use yourself, then, certainly, someone else will.

438. Most people talk without substance other than their own for immediate gain.

439. If you don't know how to say what you mean or what you want, then you don't know what you mean or want.

440. Fighting as a way of life is a negative goal.

441. When you come to see the All of no-thing, no-thing will be the completeness of All.

442. If you don't do it right the first time, you will probably do it wrong the second time.

443. I don't need what I am because of who I am; what I am is because I know who I am.

444. Hope is for the weak minded and not for the builder of empires.

445. You don't have to know how it works; you just have to know that it does.

446. The difference between positive and negative is that the positive always has it going on even when it doesn't, and the negative hasn't got it going on even when it does.

447. Smart is better than intelligent —most of the time.

448. If you can't tell one from the other, consider all aspects viable.

449. When you want something done, demand that your soul comply.

450. Don't waste time looking for things that aren't lost.

451. Be true to yourself, or you will become false to everyone else.

452. The sword is the soul of the samurai ONLY when the samurai is the soul of the sword.

453. Everyone is responsible for their own orgasm.

454. Perfect ascension does not require commitment.

455. Liberty gives one the ability to pursue what is viable for one's experiences, Freedom gives one the ability to make a wrong choice.

456. Reality is the given situation, irrespective of perception.

457. The past is always behind us when it should be before us as a reminder not to talk out of our asses.

458. Let your curses be someone's blessings.

459. There is no rhyme or reason to fate regardless of free will.

460. Remember what you learned from your teachers, but not what they taught you.

461. Accept your own perfection without rationalization.

462. A soul is required for dealing with and allaying the fears of the unknown.

463. It takes the same amount of energy to be a winner as it does to be a loser.

464. Do not confuse experience with definition.

465. You can't get there if you already are.

466. It is very difficult to be a self-starter when people keep reaching for your ignition keys.

467. Don't let your presumption cloud your reality.

468. True genius comes to bear when a man does not permit the thought to be released back to the nothingness from where it came.

469. Be prepared ... to be prepared.

470. It is not the tool ... it is the intention.

471. Fate is based on your true desire to determine the outcome of a conflict according to the extent of your own belief and faith–nothing more, nothing less.

472. Procrastination weakens intent.

473. Practice your ideal until you are the ideal itself.

474. When you come to understand your desires, the concept of failure fails to embrace any of your thoughts.

475. Martial arts and military skills are not the same. Do not confuse the conundrum.

476. If you really want to keep your stuff together, be smart enough to know you ain't smart enough.

477. Suffer the eradication of guilt and self-imposed nihilism.

478. If you have to prove you're the best, then you ain't the best.

479. The more you think about something, the less you are that.

480. Most things are aleatory; we prefer to think there is a reason for everything so we can satisfy our inconsequence.

481. Where you are is what you need.

482. Why insist on being when it is simpler to just be as is?

483. If something is gonna happen, it happens and does not need negotiation.

484. Always be what you left for.

485. Backing down is sometimes required as you prepare to move up.

486. Respect the target of your derision.

487. Leadership without sanction is like farting in a wind storm.

488. Self-reliance is being able to rely on others to maintain the self.

489. True love is the result of, not the preface to.

490. Fate is not our responsibility to determine: that emanates from a higher mind; choice is a self-perpetuated myth.

491. Better to be called a scoundrel than to be mourned over.

492. Beware false platitudes of clever gratitudes.

493. What's meant to be simply is and doesn't have to find a way.

494. If you're not going to be real, you can't be make-believe.

495. Honor is something you are, not something you attain.

496. It is your intention that brings about deliverance, not your well-meant practice.

497. It is not the food on the plate as much as it is the anticipated taste based on the platter arrangement.

498. It's a bitch to be a bitch, moreso when you think it is and even if you don't.

499. Most people kill the goose that laid the golden egg because they cannot deal with uncommonality.

500. Illusion exists on a plane that you don't.

501. Count your money, not your mantras. It's a physical world.

502. Don't be afraid of knowing that you know, but only when you do know that you do know.

503. Energy will always go in the direction of your intention.

504. Be expubediantly prodigious.

505. Meditation ensures procrastination.

506. You can't understand mortality until it becomes a tangibility in your mind.

507. Preclusion is intrusion as conclusion is delusion.

508. See beyond the cube of all in non-dimensional realities.

509. It is not hard to be me; it is hard being me.

510. When you must reckon with something, make sure that it doesn't wreck on you.

511. Never presume to know what a master is thinking until you are a master of *that* discipline.

512. If you can't explain what you want in 25 words or less, you don't know what you want.

513. **Difficulties in life lie in being unable to accept yourself as complete and perfect without having to practice**

514. You can't close if you don't open.

515. If you insist on playing with your petunia make sure it is strong enough to withstand the tug.

516. If you want to be perfect, accept your perfection and you'll be perfect.

517. Being bigger than life is the result of people not letting you be who you are, but rather wanting you to be what you are.

518. Trying to do something and actually doing it is the difference between wanting and having.

519. A muse you use to inspire you, not perspire you.

520. When you learn a technique – abandon it – and it will be what it presupposes.

521. Do you know what happens when you die? Nothing! You don't.

522. Be two-faced at all times so no one knows where you're at except yourself and maintain a disavowal of fearing yin and yang.

523. Poor should not be without its own dignity.

524. When you die, you leave behind you a great inconvenience: it is best to merely transition with emptiness.

525. Anyone with a weapon can think they are a warrior, which is not to be confused with being a warrior and needing no arms.

526. Do what you deem necessary for the propagation of your own mythology.

527. Annihilate the authority of good and evil and so what is correct for circumstance.

528. IT is the abyss of the finite that is infinity.

529. The abolition of desire is based on acceptance; acknowledgement of having and not wanting making pursuance a needless exertion.

530. Sense your own joy of being or become a walking irrelevancy.

531. Patience and prudence are two of the greatest sucker punches ever perpetrated on the human psyche in the Parthenon of failure.

532. That's it! What do you want for $12.95?

About the Author

Stephen F. Kaufman is a world renowned martial arts master, an authority on management strategy and reality facilitation, and is the author of the best-selling interpretations of *Musashi's Book of Five Rings, Sun Tzu's Art of War, Lao Tzu's Living Tao, The Shogun Scrolls, The Sword in the Boardroom, Zen and the Art of Stick fighting*, and the Hanshi David Mann action adventure novels.

He has penned more than 37 books and short stories. His work is considered essential study for individuals and organizations interested in progressive management and motivation development that includes life enhancement skills.

As an ordained minister, he is the founder and master of the Self-Revealization Acceptance™ movement and is the author of *Self-Revealiza'tion Acceptance™ - Your Divine Right to Live in Joy and Freedom and Practicing Self-Revealization Acceptance - 52 Weekly Ascensions to Empower Your Life*, the first, foremost, and original reality facilitation concept ever presented to the modern world in 1993, and guaranteed to bring immediate and permanent results.

Titles by Stephen F. Kaufman

HWP

Hanshi Warrior Press
"…words that matter"

Hanshi Warrior Press focuses on books of merit that convey works of realistic spiritual ascension, freedom of thought and innovation in the worlds of Universal philosophy, martial arts, life strategy, business management, motivation, and fiction.

81347324R00078

Made in the USA
Columbia, SC
29 November 2017